For Valerie

TAK[E TIME]
FOR
YOURSELF

MEDITATIVE MOMENTS
FOR HEALTHY LIVING

RUTH FISHEL

Illustrations by Bonny Van de Kamp

*For Special
Time for you!*

*With
Love &
Peace
Ruth*

Health Communications, Inc.
Deerfield Beach, Florida

For up-to-date information on Ruth Fishel's retreats, advances, workshops, conferences and tapes, or to be on her mailing list, write to:

Ruth Fishel
Spirithaven
17 Pond Meadow Drive
Marstons Mills, MA 02648
Or call or fax: 1-508-420-5301

©1995 Ruth Fishel
ISBN 1-55874-368-5

Publisher: Health Communications, Inc.
3201 S.W. 15th Street
Deerfield Beach, Florida 33442-8190

Cover design by Ileana M. Wainwright

Contents

✤

Acknowledgments

This book was originally printed in the form of four little booklets. I was thrilled when the first two printings sold right out, and I would like to thank all the readers who took the time to write or call and let us know how much they liked the booklets. Your encouragement inspires me to keep writing and that feels wonderful!

Thank you, Peter Vegso, publisher of Health Communications, Inc., for having the vision to combine the mini-books into one larger book and for continuing to publish books that help lift our spirits.

Thank you, Christine Belleris, my editor, for being so easy and enthusiastic to work with. Thanks, Ileana M. Wainwright, for your wonderful cover. A special thank you to Bonny Van de Kamp for your wonderful talent and your terrific art. And to my partner Sandy Bierig, for her editing, ideas, support, patience and loving attention to my work.

Dear Reader

❧

It's time for you! Doesn't that feel good? It's time to take time for yourself, to get in touch with yourself, to make peace with yourself and to think well of yourself.

Do you really know what you want in life? Or from life? Do you really know what matters most, and how you go about getting it?

You might think you want money, prestige, fame or the prettiest gal or most handsome guy. You might think you want a big house or a big job or a big bank account. You might think that when you get these things you'll be happy. But look below that. Look a bit deeper. Do you think these "things" will bring you peace of mind, joy, security, comfort, health, love? When you have these "things," what next? Will you have a sense of fulfillment or accomplishment? And how long will those feelings last?

After working with others in their spiritual quest, I have found that most people, when they look deeply within, have relatively simple wants. After their basic needs for food and shelter are satisfied, they finally get in touch with their deepest needs: to love and be loved, to belong, to be able to get in touch with and express their creativity, to know their lives have a purpose.

The bottom line is we really want to feel good inside. We want to have loving relationships. Most of us want a primary partner or marriage relationship. Most of us would like financial security. We know that we don't want to have fear, pain, pressure, insecurity and a myriad of other things that make us feel unhappy or uncomfortable. Unfortunately, these are all a part of the package of life. We can't stop these feelings when life happens to us in ways that are not to our liking.

However, we can maximize the time when we do feel comfortable and at peace; and, we can minimize the time we are in struggle and pain. We can do this by first taking time for ourselves!

Each of us does belong. We simply have to stop long enough to find that out. If we are always looking outside for what we want to do next, we'll never feel good about ourselves. We have to stop and nurture ourselves, to get to know ourselves and, yes, even to pamper ourselves. If we don't know who we are, we can't know what we need. And if we can't make peace with ourselves, how can we ever like ourselves or the lives that we live?

So this book is all about giving yourself permission to be just who you are, to be gentle with yourself, and to honor yourself and your process, and even to pamper yourself.

It's about
Taking time for yourself,
Thinking well of yourself,
Making peace with yourself,
and
Getting in touch with yourself.

I hope you enjoy the journey!

With love,

Ruth Fishel

Part I

Take Time
for
Yourself

self esteem

Take time to come home to yourself everyday.

Robin Casarjean

A Time to Be Selfish

There comes a time . . . or two . . . or many . . . in our lives when we are given the gift of awareness. It is a time when we are able to recognize where we really are in this moment of life, having nothing to do with where we want to be, where we would rather be or where we think we ought to be.

And, when this gift is combined with acceptance, accepting this moment in time, we are very blessed.

There comes a time . . . or two . . . or many . . . in our lives when we are in a place where we can recognize and accept how very needy we are, or how much we hurt or how very lonely we might be. This recognition can happen after a great change. It can happen when we are aware of the grace of God working in our lives. It often happens after a life-changing event or when we are facing a change.

Change always includes a loss, a giving up of one thing for something else. It can happen at a time when we have given up something that might have served us well at one time.

We face pain when we are ready to let go of our blocks and are willing to see what we have been hiding. We face pain when we are willing to find the courage to peek under our anger to find its true source. We face pain when we find the courage to share our guilt and shame in order to find our freedom.

We are in pain when we have lost a loved one or been hurt badly so that our boundaries have been bulldozed.

Whatever the reason for our pain, it does not matter. What matters is that we see we have a need.

We must take time to get our basic needs met. We must do this. We cannot be good for anyone else until we are good to ourselves.

It's okay to think of ourselves first. In fact, there comes a time in our lives when we must do so.

me!

On the following pages you will find healing inspirational words and thoughts. Let the words touch you . . . embrace and soothe you. Let the words inspire you and help you to be gentle with yourself. Let yourself be inspired to action or, if it fits your needs, inspired to non-action . . . to rest. Let these words help you in the process of healing and feeling good about yourself. Let them help you build your self-esteem and a sense of your life's purpose.

There is no order that needs to be adhered to, no rhyme or reason in the way the pages are presented. You can read a section or a page a day, a section or page at random or the entire book in a sitting.

But stop and take the time to let the words sink in, listen to the words with all your senses. Let the words come to life for you and soothe you. Let the words sink into your mind and then let your body feel the results. Know that you deserve to take all the time you need for yourself.

You deserve a special time each and every day . . . just for you . . . to be selfish . . . to fill your needs and no one else's. It is all right.

Take time off from the responsibilities of this day for you. Not time to escape. Not mindless time to deny or push away feelings. But time to be with just what you feel, wherever you are, whatever you are feeling . . . without judgment, without resentments, without blame, without wanting to feel differently. A time to honor your feelings and come to know them and be okay with them. Give yourself permission and watch the wonderful results.

just for me!

*Today I honor this time in my life
and take time for me.*

All of us go through painful times in our lives. And it is absolutely natural to wish we could avoid them. All of us go through ups and downs, joys and sadness, times of abundance and times of need. It is a natural a part of life as rain and sunshine.

When we can accept that where we are in this moment is okay, no matter what we are feeling, we receive the gift of peace and serenity. When we accept that changing moods and circumstances are all part of the natural flow of life, we are free to move on.

Today I honor who I am,
where I am, and I give myself
permission to think
of me first.

To be truly aware of each moment and to be able to accept each moment is a goal. When we are able to achieve it, we come to a place of peace within. For most of us, those moments are rare indeed. They grow more frequent in direct proportion to our willingness to grow in that direction.

Take time to see where you are on your path to acceptance.

Be willing to pray for greater acceptance. Bring your awareness to where you are in this moment and accept with love and gentleness.

*I give myself permission for
some personal pampering today,
discovering healthy new things
that I can do for myself
to feel good.*

There is a big difference between self-nurturing, self-indulgence and self-pity. Positive action is one of the biggest differences. Indulgences of any kind that we use to deny our feelings in order to feel better, simply leave us with those feelings at a later time. When we sit around feeling sorry for ourselves and look to other people, places or things to make us feel better, we are indulging in self-pity.

Self-nurturing is a positive action step. We stop. We look at where we are. We accept where we are. And we take some time for personal pampering, nurturing all our senses, connecting with our inner needs, and discovering the action steps that we need to take to grow and get better.

I am taking time for me today
to see myself and love
myself just as I am.

Patience

Even after taking all the action steps that we know, we might still feel unclear. There are still times in our lives when our answers are not completely clear. There are times when we know a change needs to be made but we are not sure what to do. Maybe we have done everything that has worked in the past and still have not received any answers.

If we have prayed and meditated on the subject, spoken to a friend, sponsor or spiritual advisor and still feel stuck, maybe there is more information that we need to get.

Maybe we need to wait and let more time pass.

When we have done all the footwork we can and still do not see what to do or where to go, it is time for us to develop faith and patience. We can turn a difficult time into a new lesson by learning to trust that we will know what to do or not do when the time is right to know . . . and not one moment before.

*Today I trust that my Higher Power
knows what is best for me and
will let me know when the
time is right to act.*

Time

There are times when everything we know from experience and good judgement tells us to make a certain choice. All the advice we receive from friends and trusted advisors backs this up.

And yet something in our hearts tells us to wait. Something whispers that another answer might he better for us. When this happens, it is best to wait before making a decision either way.

Wait.

Pray.

Ask for help and . . .

    wait some more.

time for me!

Trust your inner feeling and you will
know what to do.
Trust that you will know
and
you
will
know.

I begin my day today with prayer and meditation, knowing that this is my special time to connect with my Higher Power. Within the quiet and peace of this special moment I am being guided to action or waiting, to knowing or having faith and trust that I will know. Whatever answer I receive is right for me in this moment.

Too Busy Being.
Too Busy Trying
Too Hard

So many times we try to force things to happen. Think of all the energy that has gone into those times. When we make up our minds that we want certain results and will settle for nothing less, more often than not we suffer.

When we have done our footwork and are so attached to the results that nothing else is acceptable, when we think that we are the only one who knows what we should have, self-centeredness has taken over. We have forgotten there is a power greater than ourselves.

Our immature self tells us that we deserve the results that we want. Our negative self-talk won't let up and tells us to do this or that, talk to this person or that person, write this letter or make that phone call. And if none of this works, our negative self-talk tells us to go back and do it all over again.

The time and energy wasted could have gone into many other positive action steps. The aggravation and the worry just drained us from feeling peaceful and in charge of our lives.

When we feel ourselves getting agitated, it is time to . . .

Stop.
Reevaluate.
Ask for help.
Meditate.
Let go.
Wait.

letting go!

When I feel that things are not going my way, I can stop. I can ask for help and wait until I am sure what to do.

I can say the *Serenity Prayer.*

God, grant me the serenity
To accept the things I cannot change;
Courage to change the things I can, and
Wisdom to know the difference.

I can take time to ask for knowledge of God's will for me and the power to carry that through.

taking time...
to listen

A Life of Peace Does Not Mean the Absence of Conflict

Many think that to be on the spiritual path, to meditate, to follow our principles to the best of our ability, to follow a 12-step or other program of recovery and to be of service, life should flow smoothly and be full of peace and serenity.

Yes, life does flow. And there is peace and serenity. But as we have seen, there are conflicts and pain, death and disease, hurricanes and earthquakes. These are the biggies that we know we can do nothing to prevent, but we can be prepared.

As long as we are alive, there will always be things to work through.

Take some time to examine some of the following blocks to peace and serenity. And then add others of your own. Examine them without judgment. Examine them with gentleness and acceptance.

Take time to be gentle
with yourself.

pushing us off course....

Take time to think about how you react.

What do you do when . . . you feel hurt?

hurt?

When you don't get what you want?

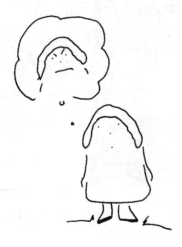

When you feel cheated, maybe even lied about?

my reactions

When your desires come into conflict
with others?

When you come in second . . . or fifth
or last . . . or can't even finish?

When you lose your temper?

When you say things that hurt someone else?

When you don't meet your own expectations?

When self-knowledge isn't enough?

We might make all kinds of discoveries that bring insight to our problems and still lack the ability to change. We might make firm decisions to let go of or give up something that we see is destructive or negative in our lives and not be able to follow through with it. Our intentions might be very powerful and we feel a strong commitment to action steps we see as necessary, and yet . . . we still feel stuck and nothing changes. There comes a time when seeing isn't enough. There comes a time when self-knowledge isn't enough. There comes a time when we feel powerless.

Once we can accept that we are powerless, we are in the process of turning a new corner on our spiritual path. Once we are ready to admit and accept that we are powerless, we are then ready to let a Higher Power into our lives.

We are opening ourselves up to be *other powered*, whether we see that power coming from God, Allah, Christ, The Power of Love, Spiritual Energy or whatever is right for us as an individual. Changes will really begin to happen and we will begin to feel lighter and to connect with a greater self-awareness and gain a new sense of direction.

Spirituality becomes a whole new way of life.

my spiritual path to new changes and possibilities

Part II

Think Well

of

Yourself

What you think of yourself is much more important than what others think of you.

—Seneca

I celebrate myself today.
I am alive. I am growing. I am
willing to do all I am able to do
to be the best of who I am.

The Healing Power of Words

Words . . . our own words that we use when we speak to ourselves and to others are powerful assets.

Whatever we are feeling in any moment can be changed instantly by the words that we use. We don't have to look anywhere else but to ourselves and to the words that we speak and the words that we think in order to feel good. We have within us, right at our fingertips this simple but powerful healing aid that we can use to be in charge of our feelings and our health.

Science now knows that our bodies and our brains are inseparable. What begins in our brain flows through our entire body. The words that we think create immediate results in the way we feel.

Words actually have the power to move our feelings from one place to another.

Words have the power to

    m
      o
        v
          e

          us

to a place

               d
               e
               e
               p
            within.

words words words to peace

We are *touched* by words.

Words can reach into our hearts.

Words can stimulate us and actually change our moods.

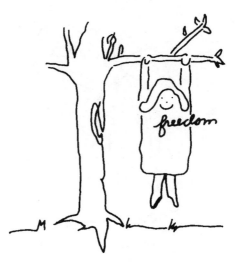

Thoughts formed into words
can spread
feelings
throughout our body.

Words Inspire

The word *inspire* means to breathe into, to infuse or arouse the mind with a feeling or an impulse that can lead to creative action, to animate or to stir. We can arouse or create a feeling or an idea or an action.

We can *inspire* ourselves. Our very thoughts move us.

We are moved by the messages that we tell ourselves, to positive or negative, healing or destructive actions and feelings. Our bodies respond with sickness or health.

It is important that we *stop* and *listen* to the way we talk to ourselves. It is important because we can change any negative messages that we give ourselves.

The words that we use can *change* how well we feel and function.
Let's try this for a moment . . .

Let yourself
feeeeeel
the effect of just one
word.

61

Spend a few moments being still and let yourself *feeel* how powerful one word can be.

Gentleness

Let yourself *feeel* how this one word

Gen-tle-ness
makes you feel.

See how it changes whatever you were feeling before you looked at that word. Can you slow yourself down enough to see what thoughts are going on in your mind? Don't judge the thoughts. Just notice the thoughts. Be aware of the thoughts that this one word can trigger in your mind.

Our thoughts, the words that we tell ourselves, trigger our feelings.

With all this in mind, this section of the book can be used in a variety of ways and you will find the right way for you. May I suggest four ways?

1. Whatever you are feeling, whatever page you open this section to, read the word, spend a moment thinking about the word, close your eyes and let the feelings pour all over your body. Bring your complete awareness to the word, the single word on the page and let your entire body be open to the results of the thought of this one word. Whatever else you might have been feeling, see how this word can change that feeling.

2. Select a particular word from the following pages that you would like to feel and use the process above.

3. Take time to be by yourself. Get yourself centered. Take a few moments to be with your breath. Bring all your attention to your breath as you breathe in and out from your nose. As your mind quiets down and you feel yourself centered, open the book at random,

see the word, close your eyes again and imagine yourself breathing in this word with every in breath. See whatever color, texture, size or shape appears for you. There are no rights or wrongs here.

Just let yourself see the word and as you breathe in this word, let whatever feelings come up for you pour all over your body, letting yourself FILL with all the feelings this word brings.

4. Now you might want to make a choice as to which word you would like to feel instead of random choosing. So spend some time with some of the words in the next few pages. Experience the power of these words. See how powerful your thoughts can become. experience and learn the power we have over our feelings and know we have the power to change how we feel.

These are just a few of many action steps we can take to learn how to improve our self-esteem . . . how to feel good about ourselves . . . and how to be in charge of our lives.

Love

Peace

peace

Abundance

abundance

Easy

70

Power

is knowing you're ok!

First things first

first things first

Easy does it

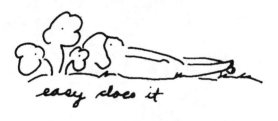

easy does it

Faith

Go with the flow

go with the flow!

Keep it simple

keep it simple

Let go, let God

Turn it over

turn it over

Caring

caring

Joy

joy!

Gentle

gentle

Soft

Strength

strength!

Healing

healing ♡

Confidence

confidence

Goodness

goodness

Enthusiasm

enthusiasm

Truth

Integrity

integrity!

Just for today

just for today

Positive change

⭐ positive change

Higher Power

Spiritual

Spiritual

Change

change

Growth

growth

Positive energy

positive energy

Healing energy

healing energy

Self-esteem

self-esteem

Expect miracles

expect miracles

Inner child

inner child

100

intuition

Trust

Nurturing

nuturing ♡

Coming home

coming home

Alive!!!

☆
alive!!!

Part III

Make Peace with Yourself

From Chaos to Peace

How many times have you felt edgy or scattered? Are there times when you are unable to concentrate and can't figure out why? Or maybe you're just not quite sure what's wrong, but you know that something certainly is. Something doesn't feel quite right but you just can't put your finger on it.

Perhaps you feel stuck. You know that if you changed something, you would feel better. But you are not able to do that and you are not really convinced that if you did make the change, it would really matter anyway.

Maybe you have already tried many things: therapy, 12-step programs, retreats, workshops, conferences, meditation. Life seems to get better for a while but then gets chaotic or undirected or painful in a short time.

If you can identify with any of the above, maybe you would like to join me on a mini-journey within. The following pages present thoughts, ideas and simple steps that work to help you to get to the source of your discomfort. They can guide you to your blocks to peace. They can help you bring peace to chaos.

But remember to bring your willingness because there is foot-work to be done.

There is an Eastern parable that describes the untrained mind as a monkey, swinging from branch to branch at whim, doing whatever it wants to do at any time. This is not only chaotic and out of control, but is stressful and the breeder of all kinds of disease (dis-ease), unhappiness and loss. An untrained mind is full of reactions and projections, jumping to everything that comes up.

This can often be experienced when we are least aware of what is going on, when we first wake up. We might suddenly feel agitated, depressed or fearful and not know how we got that way.

This continues to happen through the rest of our day. One thought leads to another thought which leads to a reaction which might lead to an action and so on and so on and so on.

We no longer have to be at the whim of our untrained mind. We no longer have to be its victim. We no longer have to feel powerless.

We can change this by practicing seven simple steps.

7 Simple Steps to Peace

1. Stop.
2. Become aware of "it," whatever "it" is that you are feeling.
3. Feel it.
4. Name it.
5. Accept it.
6. Love it.
7. Take an action step.

Now take a few moments to reflect on each step.

1. *First, we need to STOP.*

But how can we do that? What does that even mean?

You can STOP by bringing your attention to your breath.

Very gently
breathe in and breathe out.

stop for peace

2. *Awareness*.

Now bring your awareness to whatever
IT is that is going on for you in the
moment.

aware!

3. *Feel it.*

Feel whatever comes up for you in the
moment.

feeeel it!

4. *Name it.*
Make a mental note of what you feel.

5. *Accept it.*

Let go of all resistance and denial and accept fully, to the best of your ability, what it is that you are feeling.

6. *Love it.*

Give unconditional love and acceptance to whatever you see in this moment.

119

7. *And then . . .*
ACTION STEP(S) if necessary.

If you haven't found peace or release from the upset, then an action step is still necessary.

action!

"can we get together and talk?"

What Are the Action Steps That I Can Take?

There are many things that can help to release or change the feelings that are blocked. Think about what might help you.

- Write a letter to someone you have an issue with and do not mail it.
- Write a letter and do mail it.
- Call your sponsor.
- Talk to a therapist.
- Go to a meeting.
- Do a Fourth and Fifth step.
- Talk to a friend.
- Beat your pillow or take part in an active sport, such as volleyball.
- Walk or jog.
- Pray.
- Meditate.
- Turn it over.
- Give it time.

Feelings

These *7 Action Steps* work if we know what our feelings are. But it is not at all unusual to deny or to have blocked feelings.

Feelings come in all sizes, shapes, colors and density. Feelings can be healing and soothing, agitating or painful.

feelings

Sometimes feelings make us feel alive!

very alive!

Other times they are so heavy that we feel as if we are being weighed down or are carrying a burden far too heavy to bear. Sometimes they are so thick that they block us from seeing anything else.

There are times that we feel and don't know what it is that we are feeling. And other times we misinterpret our feelings. Anger can do this to us. Anger can cover up many other things that we cannot see until we *EXPEL* . . .

> *Let out . . .*
>> *Release . . .*
>>> *Get rid of . . .*
>>>> the anger.

Anger can have so many other feelings under it. It can serve as a cover-up for the feeling of powerlessness. It can tell us that we don't feel sad, and when we finally let ourselves experience our anger, we can feel overwhelmed with all the rage and bitterness that has been hidden for years.

As we grow spiritually, there are times when we are just full of feelings. This is often a most unusual state for us to be in since most of us have suppressed our feelings for years. It has been natural for us, an instinctual survival mechanism, to block our painful feelings. We might have blocked them in a number of ways, including alcohol, food, drugs, sex, depression, excitement and co-dependency. In recovery we learn that anything we block keeps us stuck. So we gradually risk getting in touch with our feelings. We become willing to give up some of the blocks and let our truth in.

127

We begin to make our own acquaintance. We begin to find out who we really are. We begin to get to know ourselves without our masks, without our blocks, without our walls and, most of all, without our mood alterers.

Some of us might recognize a feeling for the first time in many years. As this begins to happen, as we begin to let ourselves feel anything, it can be frightening. Some of the feelings will be painful and sad. But it can also feel good. It can feel alive. And naturally when something feels good, we want more of it. We want to hold on tightly to what feels good, not let it go.

We might even discover that we can do things just to keep feeling because it makes up feel so alive.

For example, anger can stimulate the adrenaline. We can enjoy the feeling and stay mad, unwilling to work things through, unwilling to give up this natural high.

And self-pity can feel natural. We have felt bad for ourselves for so many years, we might want to hold on to this feeling and continue to feel this way because we deserve it.

As we begin to allow ourselves to have our feelings, as we learn how to watch them and get to know them, we learn that feelings don't stay. They move on to make room for other feelings to come in. By having our feelings and getting to know them, we will see that they will fade out and pass on. New feelings will move in, fade and pass on so that newer feelings from newer experiences can come in. We just learn to go with the flow, no longer controlled by our feelings.

In our search for inner peace, we have to continue to look within ourselves for those answers. Here are some questions we can ask ourselves as we continue on this journey within. In this process of self-examination, trust that you are in the process of discovering new ideas which will lead you to your next step.

What are the things that keep me from feeling peaceful?

fear, anger, drugs, hate, pride????

what are my roadblocks?

What do I want?

what do i want?

peace, happiness, candy, booze,
education, food, friends, lovers,
travel, degree, children,
status, things ......?

What do I need?

what do i need
need
need
need
need!

Where do I react physically to upset in my body?

What do I do with my anger?

What is my immediate reaction when someone or something upsets me?

Do I have someone I can talk to when I feel upset?

Is there an action step I need to take to become free?

Feelings Connected with Action Steps

In our attempt to feel pleasure and avoid pain at all costs, we are often tempted to take action steps that bring immediate gratification and long-term suffering. Most of us have had years of training in rationalization and denial, so it is often difficult to look beyond immediate gratification.

Certain action steps lead to predictable feelings when we get to know ourselves better. And self-knowledge leads to wisdom which leads to peace and contentment. The next time you choose to take an action step that is questionable, when a small voice inside asks if this is really the thing to do, try using an emotional thermometer first.

Insight Checklist.

Emotional Thermometer.

When we are not feeling well physically, it's common for a doctor to take our temperature, check our pulse and blood pressure. She might even press different parts of our body, looking for deeper signs of pain or trouble. X-rays and other tests may be ordered so she can gather additional information to make an intelligent diagnosis.

In a similar fashion we can learn to examine our own feelings so we can make intelligent decisions on action steps in our lives.

When something comes up for you that you want to explore further, try the following Insight Checklist.

When making a decision for an action step, take some time to visualize yourself taking that action. Sit quietly, close your eyes very gently and visualize how you will feel as a result of this action. Follow it through from your thoughts to your feelings.

For example, if you have been trying to lose weight and suddenly had a disappointment, your first reaction might be to go out for an ice cream sundae. Immediate satisfaction but long-term pain.

Or if you have been in the process of breaking off a destructive relationship, a telephone call could result in short-term gratification and long-term pain in the prolonging of this relationship.

my feelings

So imagine an action step and examine the feelings that result.

I am now exploring taking the following action step: _____

_____

_____ .

These are the feelings that come up for me when I visualize taking this step:

_____

_____

_____

_____

_____ .

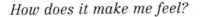
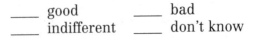

How does it make me feel?

____ good ____ bad
____ indifferent ____ don't know

What is this feeling?

____ short-term? ____ long-term?
____ I don't know

What are some healthy action steps I can take for long-term spiritual growth and change?

Here are some affirmations you can use that can help you make positive, healthy changes in your life. Look at each one and say them slowly, with feeling. And then write your own!

*I am in charge of how
I feeel today.*

*I have the power to change
how I f e e e l today.*

*Today I am noting whatever
comes up that keeps me
from feeling peaceful.*

I am bringing my awareness to all my
blocks to inner peace . . .
gently and without judgment.

*I am recording these events,
thoughts, people and places and
my reactions to them.*

How to Become Spiritually Centered Before Getting Up in the Morning

There is a very soft moment we experience between sleep and waking up. In this moment there are no thoughts. In this moment we truly do experience the moment. We gradually become aware and then . . .

BOOM!

Thoughts begin happening and, depending on the place we are in emotionally and spiritually, our body begins to respond to our thoughts. It is important to remember that our body does not know the difference between something real or something imagined.

How do we begin our day with peaceful feelings, no matter what is going on in our lives? How do we learn to become in charge of our feelings from the beginning of the day until the end of the day?

We begin with that soft, warm moment between sleeping and waking.

We begin by bringing our attention to the moment and noting, not resisting, what is going on in the moment.

As you become aware that you are awake, gently notice whatever thoughts are going through your mind.

Gently notice your reactions to your thoughts.

Be with your reactions.

notice ⁛

Be with all the feelings that are taking place right now.

What were the thoughts that preceded the feelings?

Let everything be just as it is and notice the feelings pass by.

Gently bring your attention to your breathing.

Breathe in deeply through your nose and softly say to yourself, *"Good Morning"* and then add *your name.*

Breathe in deeply through your nose.

Know that every time you breathe in you are freeing more and more endorphins (natural energy boosters) to flow through your body.

155

Every time you breathe in, you release all your endorphins to flow throughout your body, energizing, soothing and healing you.

Feel your breath entering your nose.
Follow it as it goes completely into your
  body . . .
Filling your chest . . .
Flowing through your shoulders . . .
Feel it flowing through your arms and
  wrists, your hands and your fingers.
Feel it flowing down your back . . . and
  into the small of your back,
down into your hips and your legs and
  into your feet.
Feel the *energy* of your *endorphins*!

energy galore

156

Know that you are NOW being filled with positive, loving, healing energy.

You are *now* being filled with loving energy.

You are *now* connecting with all the healing powers of the universe.

You are *now* being nurtured and loved.

You are *now* at peace.

And you can return to these feelings anytime during the rest of your day.

any time!

Part IV

❧

Get in Touch with Yourself

Meditation

Meditation is the quieting of our minds.

Meditation is the bridge between our outside world and our inside world.

Meditation teaches us the Spirit/Mind/Body connection. Meditation makes it possible for us to quiet down so that we can know God's will.

Meditation is simply a quieting down of our thoughts, a settling down of our mind.

It is important to know:

You can't meditate wrong!

I Choose to Meditate Today

Meditation is a great tool to help us to:

Take time for ourselves, think well of ourselves, make peace with ourselves and get in touch with ourselves.

Meditation works! It brings us peace and serenity, insight, truth and wisdom. It is our spiritual connection. Countless numbers of people have made this discovery. And yet so many, *knowing* all this to be true, do not make meditation a regular part of their daily lives.

Maybe you, like many others, meditate sporadically or for a few minutes, get something from it, yet do not meditate longer or more often.

162

Why? If meditation is such a powerful tool, why doesn't everyone meditate?

Whether you are a person who has never meditated or has a little or a lot of experience, this book can be helpful *but only if you want it to be.*

Perhaps you have meditated at some time but found little or no value in it in the past and now would like to try it again.

Or perhaps you meditate once in a while . . . when things get rough . . . and forget to do it when things go well.

busy, confused ?

Maybe you are disorganized or your life, like all of ours can be at times, feels confused and too busy. You haven't the time or the space or the privacy. Maybe you think there is too much noise or too little space or you have too many children or your children are too young or you are all alone and feel too depressed. Maybe you would have meditated more if you had seen colored lights or had a psychedelic or out-of-body experience.

Or maybe you just lack self-discipline.

Whatever your reason, whatever your experience or lack of experience, meditation can change your life. If you would like to begin the path of daily meditation, let's take time to look at some of the blocks that keep us from doing good things for ourselves and then let's learn some tools that work.

As soon as you know that you can't do your meditation wrong, you are on your way to becoming a daily meditator.

thinking about my blocks.

Regular Meditators Still Experience Resistance

This comes up for everyone once in a while and is very normal. It can help to bring new awareness to any resistance. It can help you in those times when your mind gets so busy, your forget to come back to your breath and you think you have meditated wrong.

Know that there is nothing wrong with you when you don't feel like meditating.

*And remember . . . you cannot
meditate wrong.*

Let's explore some of the reasons we use to keep us from meditating.

Join me whether you meditate regularly, occasionally, rarely or never, whether you are familiar with Insight Meditation (also known as Vipassana or Mindfulness) or have used Centering, Contemplative, Transcendental or any other type of meditation.

Looking within for our own personal answers to this question can be profoundly enlightening.

my reasons ... my blocks

Why Do We Avoid What Is Good for Us?

Wherever you are on your meditation path, take a few moments to reflect on the list below and identify with the reasons that fit you personally.

Not enough time	Boredom
Procrastination	Fear
Lazy	Lack of discipline
Doubt	Doesn't work
Too busy	Can't concentrate
Mind too active	No space

Stumbling Blocks to Meditation

For thousands of years meditators have experienced stumbling blocks to their meditation. Therefore you are not unique when you resist meditating.

By turning these stumbling blocks into stepping stones, they can be a valuable tool for self-knowledge. Bring your awareness to your resistance. Watch how you react to whatever comes up. Let go of all judgment. There is no right or wrong here.

love

I am accepting what comes
up in my thoughts and my feelings
today as I learn to love myself
for all of me . . . just the
way I am.

i'm ok!

By closely examining how we react to the different characteristics of our resistance, we grow in discipline. For example, if we think we are too sleepy to meditate and meditate anyway, we can bring this lesson to the mainstream of our lives. When we think we are too sleepy to go to work or study or pay bills or clean the house, we learn that we can do these things in spite of our self-talk.

By bringing our attention to what we are feeling, the feeling loses its power over us.

*Today I am turning my resistance
into a lesson for growth. I am growing
in strength and self-control as
I honor my commitment to
meditate today.*

i still can do it!

Discipline

M. Scott Peck says that laziness is the opposite of love and that self-discipline is usually love translated into action.

Discipline means doing something that you *choose* to do, putting immediate gratification aside for long-term rewards. Discipline means making a decision and sticking to it no matter what comes up.

As I watch any resistance
that might come up for me today,
I let it strengthen my commitment to
my meditation practice. I am at choice
today. I feel power as I choose to
be responsible for my life.

meditation

Desire for Sense Pleasures

Many of us went to great lengths to chase pleasure in order to block unhappiness. Rather than experiencing our feelings, we tried to change them through chemicals, food, people or activities.

When an unpleasant feeling or thought occurs about meditation, just be with it. If you can stay with that which you don't like, it will lose its power over you. It will go away and make room for something more pleasing to come in.

Today just as night gives
way to day and one season to another,
I can be with whatever is, knowing
that feelings and thoughts change
when I let go of my resistance to them
and just accept them the
way they are.

my feelings can change

It's . . . Playtime

Our immature self tells us that it's okay to go and play. After all, don't we deserve fun? Our self-talk will go to any lengths to look for a good time or avoid pain. It rationalizes to avoid doing things that take discipline.

Of course we deserve to have a good time. But when that is all that we chase, we will never find contentment. Peace and contentment come from within, and that can only be found when we are quiet.

I no longer need to avoid the uncomfortable or painful. I can face what comes up for me and walk through it.

We Think We Will Be Happy When We Find "It"

At the beginning of meditation many experience a natural high. You will think that you have found "IT," the "IT" you have looked for all your life.

It is normal, after a few days or weeks, for meditation to settle down. It will certainly change. Some days it will be up. Others down. As it loses it charm, you begin to resist it.

Just like life. Sunny, cloudy or a mixture.

*As I learn to experience
the flow of change, letting go of
my need for highs, giving up my
resistance to the lows, I am learning
to find a middle path and feel
peace in my acceptance.*

taking a middle path

Fear

Sometimes we let fear keep us from meditating. We fear discovering the secrets we have blocked even from ourselves. We don't want to look. We don't want to know.

Just know that whatever comes up is for your higher good. If it seems negative or destructive, it is time to see that it is, then feel it and release it. Know that whatever it is that you are denying or not dealing with is holding you back.

*Today I have all the faith I need
to look within. There is nothing
that my Higher Power and I
cannot handle.*

my higher power can

Making a Commitment

Many of us had difficulty keeping commitments. After repeated attempts at making and not keeping commitments, we began to experience a fear of making promises. We relived our past feelings of guilt when we broke our promises and fear we will feel that way again. So what do we do? We go into avoidance. Rather than take a chance of feeling bad, we go to the opposite extreme and decide never to make another commitment.

*Today my Higher Power
is filling me with energy and
enthusiasm to fulfill my commitment
to meditate. I merely need to be
willing and I am receiving all
the motivation I need.*

Fear of Failure

We miss out on a lot of good things by making extreme choices to protect ourselves from bad feelings. We say no to good things because we are afraid we will feel badly if we don't follow through. We stop taking risks. We stop growing.

One way of making this change gently is making a commitment for just five minutes a day, one day at a time. We can do almost anything for only five minutes. Even if we hate the thought.

Today I am willing to
make a commitment that I can
keep with the help of my Higher Power.
I am willing to meditate for at
least five minutes today.

Yard by Yard It's Hard.
Inch by Inch It's a Cinch.

Meditation is a good place to practice making and keeping commitments. As we experience the benefits of meditation, we increase the time we practice.

With our Higher Power, commitments become easier. When we discover that the power does not begin with us, that we are a channel for God's power to work through us, life gets much lighter, one commitment at a time.

*God is giving me all the
energy and direction that I need
to meditate without resistance today.
I am open to being a channel
for God's power.*

But I Have Too Many Thoughts. My Mind Is Too Busy.

It is absolutely normal to have thoughts. Just notice them and go back to your breathing. By experiencing them, watching them as if you were an observer, your thoughts will just be there and then go away. Whatever you observe—noise, thinking, planning, worrying, feelings, pain, self-pity—just bring your awareness to it, name it, accept it and go back to your breathing.

*As I observe the thought
processes of my mind, I am growing
in self-knowledge and self-acceptance.
I am beginning to see that thoughts
come in and go out, and only
I can give them power.*

You Can't Meditate Wrong!

As soon as you know this truth, then meditation takes on a whole new meaning. Everything that comes up for you in your meditation is what is real for you in that moment. Whether it is a thought, a feeling, an itch, a noise or the moments of peace that you so long for, that is what your meditation is about in that moment. It cannot be wrong. It is only what is. The reality of that moment is in that time and space.

Meditation Is a Practice

Just as the ballerina, the ball player and the concert pianist practice daily to develop their skills before they perform, so we sit and practice, bringing our awareness to what is going on in the moment so that we can take this skill with us.

We develop new skills when we do our practice. Soon these skills become habits and a subtle change happens in our lives. There is more calm, less stress, less reacting.

*Today I am developing skills
that improve the quality of my life
mentally, physically and
spiritually.*

*developing skills
and inner beauty*

Meditation When You Don't Want to Meditate

There will be many a morning when you get up, groan and want to turn over in bed for just five extra minutes. Your self-talk will make that perfectly justifiable for you. It might tell you that you don't need to meditate today. Or just one day skipped won't matter. Then if this doesn't work, it might tell you that meditation doesn't work anyway so why should you waste your time on such absurdity.

Sloth

Waking up in the morning is a good time to be aware of the laziness in all of us. As soon as you become aware of that part of you that really wants to sleep and will tell you anything to convince you, just recognize that you have made a commitment and accept without judgment that very human part of you that is lazy. Bring your awareness to the thoughts that precede the feelings, ask for help and get out of bed.

*Today I know my self-talk is
just looking for an easier, softer way.
I have all the energy I need today
to stay on my spiritual path
and improve my conscious contact
with God in prayer and
meditation.*

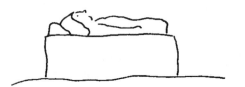

The Stumbling Blocks
of Judgment and Comparison

As we become more aware of our self-talk, we will hear excuses such as . . .

"They (the ever-present *they*) meditate better than me."

"I'm not good enough."

"I am doing it wrong."

Each one of us meditates exactly as we meditate. It is a personal discipline. No one can tell us whether it is right or wrong. Therefore we don't need to make these judgments.

*Today I smile as I hear my
negative self-talk compare and
judge. I realize and accept that my
meditation is perfect just the way
it is and I am doing exactly what
I need in this moment.*

Restlessness

Restlessness, the inability to sit quietly, can come from a number of reasons. It always begins in the mind, with our self-talk. Even before we sit to meditate, we find ourselves thinking about all the other things that need to be done, not just those things that could be accomplished during meditation.

Irritation and agitation build as we tell ourselves that we have no time for meditation, that we *should* be doing something else.

Today I accept all the restlessness and irritability that comes up for me in meditation, knowing that once I accomplish this acceptance, peace follows.

peace will follow!

Doubt

Doubt is one of the strongest stumbling blocks to meditation. Our self-talk interferes. We hear:

"This isn't working."

"It might work for others but not for me."

"It worked last week but it doesn't work now."

"It will never work."

Know that you are not alone and simply be with your doubt, examining what it feels like and how you react to it. Sit with it and let it be.

And Still More Blocks

Procrastination (I'll do it tomorrow) and other excuses such as . . .

"I don't need to. I am very healthy and well-adjusted."

"I'm too sick."

Now that excuses are over, at least for the moment, you have learned that even if you have an excuse, you don't have to give in to it. You can notice it and move on.

If you wish, you can record the following guided meditation and play it back until you can do it without the tape. Give yourself the gift of these few moments. It can be for a reward, an exercise of discipline, a treat, a break or for no reason at all but . . .

for peace . . .
   and love . . .
      for yourself!

A Gentle Basic
Meditation

Please close your eyes very . . . very
. . . gently.

And spend a few minutes . . . bringing
your *full* attention to your breath . . . as
it goes in and out from your nose.

Just be with your breath as it goes in
and out . . .

Now bring your *full* attention to the
top of your head and feel relaxation
flowing *all* over your scalp . . . Relax
your forehead . . . and bring relaxation
to the muscles around your eyes.

Feel relaxation flowing through the
bones and muscles of your face . . .
especially along your jaw. Feel the soft-
ness of your mouth as it gently closes.

Relax your throat . . . and let all your
stress . . . all your tension . . . pour down
the back of your neck . . . down through
your shoulders . . . down through your
arms . . . wrists . . . hands . . . feel all

your stress . . . all your tension . . . and anxiety . . . pouring into your fingers . . . then leaving your body through your fingertips.

Now bring relaxation to your chest . . . down through your diaphragm . . . Relaxation flowing through all the knots of your stomach . . . Feel your tension flowing . . . all the way down your spine . . . Down through your hips . . . buttocks . . . thighs . . . Tension flowing down through your knees . . . ankles and feet . . . and leaving through the tips of your toes . . .

Now breathe in relaxation to any part of your body that still feels uptight.

Now bring *full* attention back to your breathing . . . as you breathe in and out through your nose.

Notice your breath . . . whether it is warm or cool . . . whether you feel it more on one side of your nose than the other . . . Accept it just as it is. Is it deep? Or shallow. Rough or smooth? Can you feel it on the skin outside your nose?

Get to know all the characteristics of your breath for the next few minutes. As thoughts come in . . . just notice them . . . Without judging whether they are right or wrong . . . just notice them . . . and VERY gently go back to your breathing.

It is very normal to have thoughts. We all have them. Thoughts . . . feelings . . . physical pain . . . itches . . . giggles.

Planning, past memories, emotions . . . all will come up as a natural process of this meditation. Just accept what you see and feel and hear. Notice it. Bring *only* your awareness to it. Then easily and effortlessly go back to your breathing.

Follow your breath as it begins to come in to your nose, as it is going in, until it is completely in.

Then follow it as it begins to go out, as it is going out, until it is completely out.

Spend a few minutes now . . . quietly meditating. Quietly bringing your full attention to your breathing. Every time you breathe in . . . you are breathing in *powerful positive* energy . . . As you breathe out you are letting go . . . letting go of all negativity . . . tension . . . anxiety . . . making space for more positive energy to come in.

Spend a few minutes bringing your full attention to your breathing. Know that whatever comes up is perfect. Just very gently, without judgment . . . continue to come back to your breath.

Always come back to your breathing when anything takes you away from it. Stay in this place for as long as you wish and when you are ready, count to five and then very gently open your eyes.

About the Author

❧

Ruth Fishel, M.Ed., L.M.H.C., C.A.C.A.D., is author of many books, including *Time for Thoughtfulness, Time for Joy, Healing Energy, 5 Minutes For World Peace . . . Forever, Learning To Live In The Now* and *The Journey Within*. She writes and presents workshops and retreats throughout the country. She is co-founder of *Spirithaven of Cape Cod*, a healing program for women in personal growth and recovery.

Other Books by Ruth Fishel &
Health Communications, Inc.®

Time for Joy
Daily Affirmations
Ruth Fishel takes you through a calendar year with joyful quotations, thoughts, and healing, energizing affirmations.

Code 4826 . . . . $6.95

Time for Thoughtfulness
*A Daily Guide to Filling the World with Love, Care
and Compassion*
A daily thoughtfulness guide complete with inspirational quotations, uplifting thoughts and heartwarming affirmations.

Code 3227 . . . . $7.95

The Journey Within
A Spiritual Path to Recovery
A book leading you from dysfunction to the place within where your wounded being can grow healthy and strong, the place where miracles happen.

Code 4826 . . . . $8.95

Learning to Live in the Now
6-Week Personal Plan to Recovery
Enjoy today without worrying about the future or regretting the past. There is only this moment. Savor it with this loving book.

Code 4621 . . . . $8.95